Dorothy Y. Revak

October 22, 2002

Published by Barbour Books, an imprint of Barbour Publishing, Inc., P.O. Box 719, Uhrichsville, Ohio 44683, www.barbourbooks.com

ecpa Member of the
Evangelical Christian
Publishers Association

Printed in China.
5 4 3 2 1

Merry Christmas

Ellyn Sanna

Christmas is a season full of traditions—
decorations, bells, stars, a special Child—
and, most of all, happiness.
May your Christmas be filled with joy.

I wish you a
very merry Christmas!

CONTENTS

We are not simply at the mercy of the hopeless and often bad experiences that we have in the everyday world. These do not ultimately determine what we are and what we may become. New and unexpected things can always rise up out of our lives because there is, despite all the anxiety and unhappiness that surround us, a hidden source of salvation. . . . Something that is bright and pure and not simply superstitious or wildly enthusiastic is proclaimed in this Christmas. . . . Despite all the evidence that exists in the world as we know it, there is a way from darkness into light: There is a light shining in the darkness of the night.

LADISLAUS BOROS

May all the traditions of
a merry Christmas
point your heart to light.

I

Deck the Halls

Deck the halls with boughs of holly
Falalala-lalala

English Christmas Carol

When Christmas-tide
comes in like a bride,
With holly and ivy clad. . .

17TH-CENTURY POEM

A bride decorates herself for her wedding day with lace and silk and jewelry—and at Christmas, we decorate our homes and communities with evergreens and lights. Just as the bride prepares herself for the groom, we prepare ourselves for Jesus. And like the bride, we take joy in our decorations. They help to make our hearts merry.

But give me holly, bold and jolly,
Honest, prickly, shining holly;
Pluck me holly leaf and berry
For the days when I make merry.

CHRISTINA GEORGINA ROSSETTI

The holly and the ivy
When both are full well grown,
Of all the trees that are in the wood,
The holly bears the crown.

The holly bears a berry
As red as any blood,
And Mary bore sweet Jesus Christ
To do poor sinners good.

ENGLISH FOLK CAROL

Forgetting the deeper meanings at the root of our symbols and traditions, many of us connect holly with Christmas without going any further. But for people in the Middle Ages, the bright red berries and green leaves of the holly tree stood out against the cold snow, a promise of life in the midst of winter. They connected the red berries with Christ's blood, shed that we might have life as everlasting as the holly's green leaves, and they considered the points on the holly leaves to parallel the crown Christ will wear when He comes for us again.

Green grow'th the holly
So doth the ivy;
Though winter blasts
blow ne'er so high,
Green grow'th the holly.

Green grow'th the holly,
So doth the ivy;
The God of life can never die,
Hope! saith the holly.

16TH-CENTURY POEM

Be links no longer broken;
Be sweet forgiveness spoken,
Under the Holly Bough.

CHARLES MACKAY

This year, as you celebrate Christmas,
may every holly branch you see
remind you of the Christ Child,
the true Root of any merry Christmas.

II

CHRISTMAS BELLS

I heard the bells on Christmas Day
Their old, familiar carols play.
And wild and sweet
The words repeat
Of peace on earth, good–will to men!

HENRY WADSWORTH LONGFELLOW

Ring out, ye bells!
All Nature swells
With gladness of
the wondrous story,
The world was lorn,
But Christ is born
To change our sadness into glory.

PAUL LAWRENCE DUNBAR

It is the calm and solemn night!
A thousand bells ring out and throw
Their joyous peals abroad and smile
The darkness, charm'd and holy now!
To night that erst no name had worn,
To it a happy name is given
For in that stable lay new-born
The peaceful Prince of Earth and Heaven,
In the solemn midnight
Centuries ago.

ALFRED DOMMETT

When Henry Wadsworth Longfellow wrote the words of his famous Christmas carol, "I Heard the Bells on Christmas Day," America was in the midst of its bloodiest war. Longfellow's own son had been wounded at the Battle of Gettysburg six months before, and the peal of Christmas bells seemed like a mockery.

In our world today, we too have faced danger and unspeakable loss. The peace of Christmas seems far away and impossible. The thunder of bombs and the racket of machine-gun fire drown out the sound of bells.

And yet, like Longfellow, we too have reason to hope. The Christmas bells proclaim that God is still alive, still awake, still working in our world.

Then in despair I bowed my head;
"There is no peace on earth," I said,
"For hate is strong,
And mocks the song
Of peace on earth, good-will to men!"

Then pealed the bells more loud and deep;
"God is not dead, nor doth He sleep!
The Wrong shall fail,
The Right prevail,
With peace on earth, good-will to men!"

HENRY WADSWORTH LONGFELLOW

And all the bells on earth did ring,
For joy that our Saviour
He was born
On Christmas Day in the morning.

ENGLISH CAROL

Each time you hear a Christmas bell,
may your heart be filled with merriness.

III

STAR OF WONDER

Star of wonder, star of might,
Star with royal beauty bright,
Westward leading, still proceeding,
Guide us to the perfect light.

JOHN HENRY HOPKINS, JR.

Christmas is a time of starlight,
a magical time when the ordinary world steps back
so that the light of heaven can shine.
May each Christmas star you see,
whether in the sky or atop your tree,
fill you with the wonder of Christmas.

The dark night wakes,
the glory breaks,
And Christmas comes once more.

PHILLIPS BROOKS

Then be ye glad, good people,
This night of all the year,
And light ye up your candles:
His star is drawing near.

TRADITIONAL CAROL

*"We saw his star in the east
and have come to worship him."*

MATTHEW 2:2

We saw a light shine out afar
On Christmas in the morning,
And knew we straight it was Christ's star
Bright beaming in the morning.
Then did we fall on bended knee
On Christmas in the morning,
And praised the Lord who'd let us see
His glory at its dawning.

OLD ENGLISH CAROL

As Joseph was a-walking
There did an angel sing,
And Mary's child at midnight
Was born to be our King.

Then be ye glad, good people,
This night of all the year,
And light ye up your candles,
For His star it shineth clear.

OLD ENGLISH CAROL

Morning Star, O cheering sight!
Ere thou cam'st how dark the night!
Jesus mine, in me shine,
Fill my heart with light divine.

MORAVIAN HYMN

No matter how dark the night,
the star of Christmas shines on,
undimmed by human despair.
May that same star
fill your heart with light.

IV

A CHILD IS BORN

What child is this who laid to rest, on Mary's lap is sleeping?
Whom angels greet with anthems sweet,
While shepherds watch are keeping?
This, this is Christ the King,
Whom shepherds guard and angels sing:
Haste, haste to bring Him laud, the Babe, the son of Mary.

WILLIAM CHATTERTON DIX

Angels clap hands;
let men forbear to mourn;
Their saving health is come;
for Christ is born.

16TH CENTURY

Christmas is the happiest time of all the year—
for this is the birthday of Jesus, the source of all our happiness.

Rise, shepherds, though the night is deep,
Rise from your slumber's dreaming!
Jesus, the shepherd, watch does keep,
In love all men redeeming.
Hasten to Mary, and look for her Child,
Come, shepherds, and greet our Savior mild!

AUSTRIAN CAROL

How simple we must grow!
How simple they who came!
The shepherds looked at God
Long before any man.
He sees God nevermore
Not there, nor here on earth
Who does not long within
To be a shepherd first.

ANGELUS SILESIUS

A little child,
A shining star,
A stable rude,
The door ajar,
Yet in this place,
So crude, forlorn,
The Hope of all
The world was born.

ANONYMOUS

29

Christmas, the birthday of Jesus, is a time when we think of children. We relive our own childhood happiness, and we delight in the joy of the children around us today.

The innocence and wonder of childhood reveal an aspect of God—and He delights in the sound of His children's laughter on Christmas morning.

In Bethlehem is born
the Holy Child,
On hay and straw in the winter wild;
O, my heart is full of mirth
At Jesus' birth.

GEORGE FRIDERIC HANDEL

A Teenager's Memories
of Christmas

When I was little, every Christmas I would wake up at an indecently early hour. It was then my "job" to wake up my brother and sister. My sister was easy; you told her it was Christmas and that presents were under the tree—and she would hop out of bed like a jack-in-the-box. My brother, on the other hand, would get mad at us when we crept into his room and tapped him on the crown of his head (the only part of him visible from under the blankets). Most of the time he would rouse just enough to grunt at us from his nest of quilts and then turn over and go back to sleep. We quickly discovered, however, that if we pulled off all his covers, he was forced to wake up just enough to talk to us. We had to keep him talking at least four minutes before he was really awake. Otherwise, he'd go straight back to sleep.

Once we were all up, it was time to wake my parents. We would argue over who should be the one; none of us wanted to get into trouble. I, as the oldest, got the job most of the time, and I would knock tentatively on their door. Sometimes my only reward was a sleepy father yelling, "Don't come back until seven-thirty!" Other times, they were sleeping so soundly that my soft knock failed to even rouse them. Then it was on to plan B: We would have to enter their room. We would creep in and jump on them, ambushing them out of sleep. My dad would roll over and mumble, but my mom might snap, "It's only six o'clock. Go back to bed!"

My mother's word is law in our house. We would give up on our sleepy parents and creep downstairs to look at the tree, marveling at all the new packages that had arrived overnight and peeking at the interesting bulges in our stockings.

Now that I'm older, I sleep until noon any chance I get—but not on Christmas. Christmas is the one day I still wake up before anyone else in the house. I prod my sister and brother out of bed, and we hold whispered conferences about whether or not to wake my parents. I'm too big now to jump on them. . .but I have ways of waking even my heavy-sleeping father.

Some things never change. I hope they never do.

EMILY SANNA

Little Jesus of the crib,
Give us the virtues of those that surrounded you.
Make us thoughty as the fisherman,
Carefree as the drummer,
Merry in exploring the world as the troubadour,
Eager for work as the bugler,
Patient as the spinner,
Kind as the donkey,
Strong as the ox that keeps you warm.

OLD FRENCH PRAYER

Though He be Lord of all,
The Christ Child is but very small.
Kneel then and at His cradle lay,
Most gentle love
this Christmas Day.

ANONYMOUS, 14TH CENTURY

May Christ be at the center of
all your Christmas joy.

V

I WISH YOU
A MERRY CHRISTMAS

Good tidings we bring to you and your kin,
Good tidings for Christmas and a happy New Year.

TRADITIONAL ENGLISH CAROL

At Christmas,
play and make good cheer,
For Christmas comes
but once a year.

THOMAS TUSSER, 16TH CENTURY

Christmas comes only once a year—
but may you know the joy of Christmas all year long.
Each day when you wake,
may you feel a little of that
same Christmas-morning merriness.

May God bless your Christmas; May it last until Easter.

SCANDINAVIAN BLESSING

I sometimes think we expect too much of Christmas Day. We try to crowd into it the long arrears of kindliness and humanity of the whole year. As for me, I like to take my Christmas a little at a time, all through the year. And thus drift along into the holidays—let them overtake me unexpectedly—waking up some fine morning and suddenly saying to myself: "Why this is Christmas Day!" How the discovery makes one bound out of his bed! What a new sense of life and adventure it imparts! Almost anything may happen on a day like this. . . . Who knows? I may discover that this is a far better and kindlier world than I ever dreamed it could be.

DAVID GRAYSON

I wish you a merry Christmas
And a happy New Year;
A pocket full of money
And a heart full of cheer
And a great fat pig
To last you all the year.

ENGLISH TRADITIONAL BLESSING

God bless the master of this house,
Likewise the mistress too.
And all the little children, who 'round the table go.
Love and joy, come to you,
And to you, your wassail too,
And God bless you
And give you a happy New Year.

ENGLISH WASSAILERS' SONG

Without the door let sorrow lie,
And if for cold it chance to die,
We'll bury it in Christmas pie,
And evermore be merry!

ENGLISH TRADITIONAL CAROL

May your Christmas be filled with
laughter, love, a contented heart,
and the joy of Jesus.
And may you be merry,
not only at Christmas,
but your whole life long.